# THIS JOURNAL

# BELONGS TO:

# ALL ABOUT Me

## 1. What are you most grateful for in your life?

Keeping track of what you're most grateful for will keep you focused on the blessings in your life.  Consider the many reasons you have to be grateful below:

## 2. What do you love about yourself?

Self love isn't always easy but writing down what you're most proud of will help clear your mind of the criticism and negativity you may feel.

## 3. Where is your happy place?

Where do you feel most at peace?  Do you have a favorite spot that allows you to refocus your energy, find inner peace and feel happiness? Describe your happy place.

3

# ⁂ ALL ABOUT Me ⁑

## 4. What do you enjoy doing?

What are your favorite activities where you are able to boost your mood and free your mind? This could be a hobby or physical activity, or perhaps something entirely different.

## 5. Who can you rely on?

Describe the people in your life that you can count on when things get tough.  Who do you feel closest to?

## 6. How can you improve your life?

What changes can you make that will ultimately improve your life and give you joy? This could be career or personal related. Please share your thoughts below.

# ALL ABOUT Me

**7. My greatest accomplishments are:**

What are some of the things you are most proud of?

**8. What do you wish others knew about you?**

What do you wish others knew about who you really are? What do you feel others overlook?

**9. What are your greatest aspirations?**

Whether it be personal, career or family goals, list them below.

# LOVE Yourself

## STEP 1: MAKE YOURSELF A PRIORITY

It's important to always put yourself first by listening to your inner voice.
Let it guide you in eliminating toxic people and negative sources.
Don't be afraid to distance yourself from people and places that make you feel
unhappy or who don't support your journey.

## STEP 2: FACE YOUR FEARS

Don't be afraid to confront your fears
and self-doubt. Why do you feel
unworthy at times? What are you
most worried about?

## STEP 3: BE ACCOUNTABLE

Hold yourself accountable for the
things you can control and change.
There are things in your life only you
can change.

## STEP 4: FORGIVE YOURSELF

Let go of past mistakes – you can't go back in time.
We all have regrets and while it's important to hold yourself accountable for
mistakes, you can only truly heal when you learn to forgive yourself.
Free your mind so it can focus on a better you and a happier tomorrow.

## STEP 5: ACCEPT WHERE YOU ARE IN YOUR JOURNEY

Don't allow yourself to grow frustrated that you aren't able to race towards the
finish line. Your journey will take time so give yourself permission to fail
while also learning to accept where you are right now.
Take it one day at a time. You owe it to yourself to stay focused on the road ahead
while celebrating every milestone along the way.

### Write down your thoughts, reflections and ideas below:

Thoughts

# LIFE Assessment

## SUMMARIZE HOW YOU **FEEL** ABOUT YOUR LIFE

## TOP 3 AREAS OF YOUR LIFE YOU'D LIKE TO **IMPROVE**

01

02

03

## 3 WAYS YOU CAN **ACCOMPLISH** YOUR LIFE GOALS

# DEAR FUTURE Self...

FAMILY GOALS

CAREER GOALS

SELF CARE

RELATIONSHIP

HEALTH GOALS

FRIENDSHIPS

PERSONAL

FINANCIAL

TRAVEL

PASSIONS

NEW SKILLS

OTHER

5 YEARS FROM NOW

10 YEARS FROM NOW

# UNDERSTANDING Anxiety

Understanding the origin of your anxiety will help you
learn new ways to manage your responses.

**SITUATION:** Meeting
someone new

**WHAT IS YOUR BIGGEST FEAR
WHEN FACING THIS SITUATION?**

**SITUATION:** Going shopping/
to the grocery store

**WHAT IS YOUR BIGGEST FEAR
WHEN FACING THIS SITUATION?**

**SITUATION:** Stating your opinion

**WHAT IS YOUR BIGGEST FEAR
WHEN FACING THIS SITUATION?**

**SITUATION:** Standing up
for yourself

**WHAT IS YOUR BIGGEST FEAR
WHEN FACING THIS SITUATION?**

**SITUATION:** Spending time
alone with friends

**WHAT IS YOUR BIGGEST FEAR
WHEN FACING THIS SITUATION?**

**SITUATION:** Being watched
or observed

**WHAT IS YOUR BIGGEST FEAR
WHEN FACING THIS SITUATION?**

# TRIGGER Sources

**Discover what causes emotional pain
and negative thoughts in your life.**

**Describe the negative reaction/response
you would like to overcome:**

Consider the aspects of your life below and write down how each category
can cause the above trigger.

| PERSONAL | PEOPLE |
| --- | --- |
| | |

| PLACES | SITUATIONS |
| --- | --- |
| | |

Think about the different ways you can overcome your triggers
when dealing with each category.
How can you better control your reactions and manage frustrating situations?

# COPING Strategies

**Write down the different ways you feel about yourself
as well as personal situations,
and how you can better manage and cope
with self-doubt and negative feelings.**

| WHEN I'M FEELING... | I WILL MANAGE IT BY... |
|---|---|
| WHEN I'M FEELING... | I WILL MANAGE IT BY... |
| WHEN I'M FEELING... | I WILL MANAGE IT BY... |
| WHEN I'M FEELING... | I WILL MANAGE IT BY... |
| WHEN I'M FEELING... | I WILL MANAGE IT BY... |
| WHEN I'M FEELING... | I WILL MANAGE IT BY... |
| WHEN I'M FEELING... | I WILL MANAGE IT BY... |

OTHER IDEAS / NOTES

# TRANSFORMING *Thoughts*

**We all deal with negative thoughts and self-doubt.
Use this space to keep track of those feelings and focus on how
you can replace them with positive thoughts
that promote self-growth.**

| NEGATIVE THOUGHT | REPLACEMENT THOUGHT |
|---|---|
| | |

| NEGATIVE THOUGHT | REPLACEMENT THOUGHT |
|---|---|
| | |

| NEGATIVE THOUGHT | REPLACEMENT THOUGHT |
|---|---|
| | |

| NEGATIVE THOUGHT | REPLACEMENT THOUGHT |
|---|---|
| | |

| NEGATIVE THOUGHT | REPLACEMENT THOUGHT |
|---|---|
| | |

| NEGATIVE THOUGHT | REPLACEMENT THOUGHT |
|---|---|
| | |

PERSONAL REFLECTIONS

# GRATEFUL Life

What are the things you are most grateful for?
Spend time self-reflecting on the many blessings in your life.
Shift your focus on gratitude and rid yourself of
negative emotions and toxic thoughts.

| 1 | 2 | 3 |
|---|---|---|
| 4 | 5 | 6 |
| 7 | 8 | 9 |
| 10 | 11 | 12 |

# HAPPINESS Is...

**Complete the following sentences to refocus your mind
on the joys in your life:**

I FEEL MOST RELAXED
WHEN:

I AM LESS STRESSED
WHEN:

MY STRENGTHS
ARE:

I AM A GOOD FRIEND
BECAUSE:

I AM MOST
EXCITED BY:

I AM MOST FOCUSED
WHEN:

I FEEL MOST APPRECIATED
WHEN:

I AM MOST MOTIVATED
WHEN:

# SELF AWARENESS Chart

It's easy to get lost in our own headspace so it's important
that you question any negative feelings,
so you can sort through your emotions effectively.
Use this worksheet to document your progress.

THOUGHT

IS THE THOUGHT VALID?

HOW DO YOU REACT TO THIS NEGATIVE THOUGHT?

WHAT COULD YOU DO TO AVOID FEELING THIS WAY?

THOUGHTS & REFLECTIONS

# SELF AWARENESS Chart

It's easy to get lost in our own headspace so it's important
that you question any negative feelings,
so you can sort through your emotions effectively.
Use this worksheet to document your progress.

THOUGHT

IS THE THOUGHT
VALID?

HOW DO YOU REACT TO
THIS NEGATIVE THOUGHT?

WHAT COULD YOU DO TO
AVOID FEELING THIS WAY?

## THOUGHTS & REFLECTIONS

# SELF AWARENESS *Chart*

It's easy to get lost in our own headspace so it's important
that you question any negative feelings,
so you can sort through your emotions effectively.
Use this worksheet to document your progress.

THOUGHT

IS THE THOUGHT VALID?

HOW DO YOU REACT TO THIS NEGATIVE THOUGHT?

WHAT COULD YOU DO TO AVOID FEELING THIS WAY?

THOUGHTS & REFLECTIONS

# SELF Improvement

## WHAT ARE YOUR SELF SABOTAGE HABITS?

**Eliminate Negative Habits**

**Create Positive Habits**

## HOW CAN YOU IMPROVE YOUR MENTAL HEALTH?

**What Key Areas Need Work?**

**What Are Some Steps You Can Take?**

## ANALYZING THE PEOPLE IN YOUR LIFE

**Who Are The Negative Influences?**

**Who Are The Positive Influences?**

## HOW DO I HOLD MYSELF ACCOUNTABLE?

**What I Know I'm Responsible For**

**Who Helps Keep Me Accountable?**

# SELF CARE Ideas

## NURTURE YOUR MIND

Discover new hobbies

Read a book

Take a road trip

Keep a journal

Talk to a friend

Follow inspiring people

Challenge yourself

Be grateful

Call an old friend

Try something new

## FEED YOUR SPIRIT

Have "me-time"

Listen to music

Read poetry

Write "future-self"

Paint

Meditate

## TAKE CARE OF YOUR BODY

Eat healthy

Start a workout plan

Get enough sleep

Stay hydrated

Yoga

## Ideas

# SELF CARE Focus

## TOP 3 SELF-CARE ACTIVITIES

1
2
3

## HOW THEY MAKE ME FEEL

{ ☐
☐
☐

{ ☐
☐
☐

{ ☐
☐
☐

## OTHER SELF-CARE ACTIVITIES THAT MAKE ME HAPPY

01

02

03

## FAVORITE QUOTES/WORDS OF ENCOURAGEMENT

# SELF CARE Planner

**Self-care involves taking care of yourself emotionally, mentally and physically.**
**Create a self-care plan by adding activities to the categories below.**

MENTAL SELF-CARE

PHYSICAL SELF-CARE (GET ACTIVE)

EMOTIONAL SELF-CARE

DAILY HABITS (SLEEP, ETC.)

REACH OUT (SOCIALIZE)

SUPPORT NETWORK

OTHER:

# RESET YOUR mind

**We can't always control the way our thoughts,
but we can learn to transform negative feelings into positive ones
and control our reactions and impulses.
Use the chart below to start the process.**

| WHEN I FEEL LIKE: | | I WILL TRY TO CONTROL BY REACTIONS BY: |
|---|---|---|
| | } | |
| | } | |
| | } | |
| | } | |
| | } | |
| | } | |
| | } | |
| | } | |
| | } | |
| | } | |
| | } | |
| | } | |

NOTES & REFLECTIONS                    DOODLES & SCRIBBLES

# ANXIETY Levels

**Use the chart below to rate your level of anxiety when facing various situations by coloring the boxes:**

**SITUATION:** Meeting someone new

**ANXIETY LEVEL:**

**DO YOU:**        Face this fear        Avoid this situation

**SITUATION:** Going shopping or to the grocery store

**ANXIETY LEVEL:**

**DO YOU:**        Face this fear        Avoid this situation

**SITUATION:** Stating your opinion when potentially controversial or opposing

**ANXIETY LEVEL:**

**DO YOU:**        Face this fear        Avoid this situation

**SITUATION:** Standing up for yourself when treated unfairly or poorly

**ANXIETY LEVEL:**

**DO YOU:**        Face this fear        Avoid this situation

**SITUATION:** Spending time alone with friends and/or family

**ANXIETY LEVEL:**

**DO YOU:**        Face this fear        Avoid this situation

**SITUATION:** Being watched/observed when doing something/completing a task or activity

**ANXIETY LEVEL:**

**DO YOU:**        Face this fear        Avoid this situation

# ANXIETY Debrief

**Describe a situation where you felt anxious:**

**What were the physical symptoms you experienced?**

**Did you face the situation or remove yourself from it?**

**How did you cope with this anxiety?**
**Do you believe your thoughts and reactions were rational?**

# MOOD Chart

Use the wheel below to document your moods every month.
Use **3 different colors** to represent
positive, negative or neutral emotions.

POSITIVE          NEGATIVE          NEUTRAL

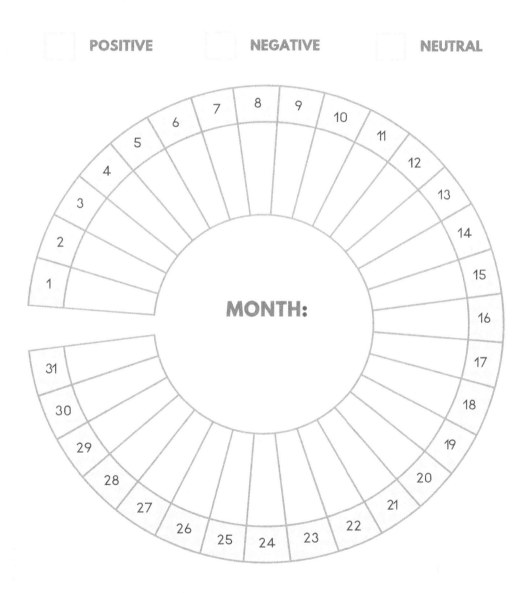

# TRIGGER Tracker

**Keep track of experiences that generate
negative thoughts and emotions.**

| DATE | INCIDENT | REACTION |
|------|----------|----------|
|      |          |          |
|      |          |          |
|      |          |          |
|      |          |          |
|      |          |          |
|      |          |          |
|      |          |          |
|      |          |          |
|      |          |          |
|      |          |          |
|      |          |          |

# SLEEP Tracker

MONTH:_____

Sleep plays a major factor in our ability to cope
with anxiety and depression.
Keep track of your sleep pattern in order to determine
how the amount of rest may be affecting your mental health.

| DAY | HOURS SLEPT | QUALITY OF SLEEP | THOUGHTS |
|---|---|---|---|
| 1 | | | |
| 2 | | | |
| 3 | | | |
| 4 | | | |
| 5 | | | |
| 6 | | | |
| 7 | | | |
| 8 | | | |
| 9 | | | |
| 10 | | | |
| 11 | | | |
| 12 | | | |
| 13 | | | |
| 14 | | | |
| 15 | | | |
| 16 | | | |
| 17 | | | |
| 18 | | | |
| 19 | | | |
| 20 | | | |
| 21 | | | |
| 22 | | | |
| 23 | | | |
| 24 | | | |
| 25 | | | |
| 26 | | | |
| 27 | | | |
| 28 | | | |
| 29 | | | |
| 30 | | | |
| 31 | | | |

# GRATEFUL Heart

| DAY | TODAY I AM GRATEFUL FOR: |
|-----|--------------------------|
| 1 | |
| 2 | |
| 3 | |
| 4 | |
| 5 | |
| 6 | |
| 7 | |
| 8 | |
| 9 | |
| 10 | |
| 11 | |
| 12 | |
| 13 | |
| 14 | |
| 15 | |
| 16 | |
| 17 | |
| 18 | |
| 19 | |
| 20 | |
| 21 | |
| 22 | |
| 23 | |
| 24 | |
| 25 | |
| 26 | |
| 27 | |
| 28 | |
| 29 | |
| 30 | |
| 31 | |

# SELF CARE Tracker

Self care is an important step in managing anxiety and depression.
It helps us recharge, reset and nurtures our mind and soul.
Focus on incorporating one self-care activity into your daily life.

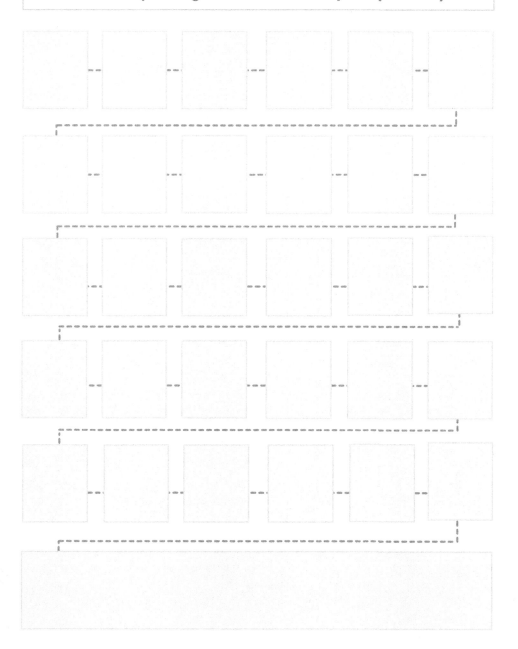

# THOUGHT Log

**Keep track of negative thoughts so you can
learn how to control irrational responses and triggers.**

| DATE | INCIDENT | INITIAL REACTION | RATIONAL REACTION |
|------|----------|------------------|-------------------|
|      |          |                  |                   |
|      |          |                  |                   |
|      |          |                  |                   |
|      |          |                  |                   |
|      |          |                  |                   |
|      |          |                  |                   |
|      |          |                  |                   |
|      |          |                  |                   |
|      |          |                  |                   |
|      |          |                  |                   |
|      |          |                  |                   |
|      |          |                  |                   |

# HAPPINESS Tracker

**Keep track of how often you feel happy and calm
and what you did to minimize negative responses.**

DATE:

DATE:

HAPPINESS RATING: ☆☆☆☆☆

HAPPINESS RATING: ☆☆☆☆☆

DATE:

DATE:

HAPPINESS RATING: ☆☆☆☆☆

HAPPINESS RATING: ☆☆☆☆☆

DATE:

DATE:

HAPPINESS RATING: ☆☆☆☆☆

HAPPINESS RATING: ☆☆☆☆☆

# PERSONAL Wins

It's important to celebrate both minor and major wins
when it comes to your mental health
and the coping  strategies you've learned along the way.
You've come a long way!

## 2 RECENT WINS

| | |
|---|---|
| | |

## TOP 3 MILESTONES

| 1 | |
|---|---|
| 2 | |
| 3 | |

## 3 THINGS I'VE LEARNED ABOUT MYSELF OVER THE LAST YEAR

| | | |
|---|---|---|
| | | |

| PERSONAL REFLECTIONS | HOW I'VE LEARNED TO COPE WITH EMOTIONS |
|---|---|
| | |
| | |
| | |
| | |
| | |

## NOTES

| |
|---|
| |
| |
| |
| |
| |
| |
| |

# PERSONAL Rewards

**Make sure to reward yourself for accomplishments
throughout your journey.
Whether it's a visit to your favorite restaurant, a bubble bath,
or an evening with friends, it's important
to celebrate your progress every step of the way.**

### IDEAS FOR PERSONAL REWARDS

| | |
|---|---|
| 1 | 2 |
| 3 | 4 |
| 5 | 6 |

| HOW I FELT BEFORE | HOW I REWARDED MYSELF | HOW I FELT AFTERWARD |
|---|---|---|
| | | |
| | | |
| | | |
| | | |
| | | |
| | | |
| | | |

| NOTES | PERSONAL REFLECTIONS/THOUGHTS |
|---|---|
| | |

# ANXIETY Tracker

MONTH:_____

## Document the days when you experienced anxiety.

ANXIETY LEVELS (1-MILD, 10 SEVERE)                    NOTES

| | | | | | | | | | | | | | NOTES |
|---|---|---|---|---|---|---|---|---|---|---|---|---|---|
| MON | 01 | 02 | 03 | 04 | 05 | 06 | 07 | 08 | 09 | 10 | 11 | 12 | |
| TUE | 01 | 02 | 03 | 04 | 05 | 06 | 07 | 08 | 09 | 10 | 11 | 12 | |
| WED | 01 | 02 | 03 | 04 | 05 | 06 | 07 | 08 | 09 | 10 | 11 | 12 | |
| THU | 01 | 02 | 03 | 04 | 05 | 06 | 07 | 08 | 09 | 10 | 11 | 12 | |
| FRI | 01 | 02 | 03 | 04 | 05 | 06 | 07 | 08 | 09 | 10 | 11 | 12 | |
| SAT | 01 | 02 | 03 | 04 | 05 | 06 | 07 | 08 | 09 | 10 | 11 | 12 | |
| SUN | 01 | 02 | 03 | 04 | 05 | 06 | 07 | 08 | 09 | 10 | 11 | 12 | |
| MON | 01 | 02 | 03 | 04 | 05 | 06 | 07 | 08 | 09 | 10 | 11 | 12 | |
| TUE | 01 | 02 | 03 | 04 | 05 | 06 | 07 | 08 | 09 | 10 | 11 | 12 | |
| WED | 01 | 02 | 03 | 04 | 05 | 06 | 07 | 08 | 09 | 10 | 11 | 12 | |
| THU | 01 | 02 | 03 | 04 | 05 | 06 | 07 | 08 | 09 | 10 | 11 | 12 | |
| FRI | 01 | 02 | 03 | 04 | 05 | 06 | 07 | 08 | 09 | 10 | 11 | 12 | |
| SAT | 01 | 02 | 03 | 04 | 05 | 06 | 07 | 08 | 09 | 10 | 11 | 12 | |
| SUN | 01 | 02 | 03 | 04 | 05 | 06 | 07 | 08 | 09 | 10 | 11 | 12 | |
| MON | 01 | 02 | 03 | 04 | 05 | 06 | 07 | 08 | 09 | 10 | 11 | 12 | |
| TUE | 01 | 02 | 03 | 04 | 05 | 06 | 07 | 08 | 09 | 10 | 11 | 12 | |
| WED | 01 | 02 | 03 | 04 | 05 | 06 | 07 | 08 | 09 | 10 | 11 | 12 | |
| THU | 01 | 02 | 03 | 04 | 05 | 06 | 07 | 08 | 09 | 10 | 11 | 12 | |
| FRI | 01 | 02 | 03 | 04 | 05 | 06 | 07 | 08 | 09 | 10 | 11 | 12 | |
| SAT | 01 | 02 | 03 | 04 | 05 | 06 | 07 | 08 | 09 | 10 | 11 | 12 | |
| SUN | 01 | 02 | 03 | 04 | 05 | 06 | 07 | 08 | 09 | 10 | 11 | 12 | |
| MON | 01 | 02 | 03 | 04 | 05 | 06 | 07 | 08 | 09 | 10 | 11 | 12 | |
| TUE | 01 | 02 | 03 | 04 | 05 | 06 | 07 | 08 | 09 | 10 | 11 | 12 | |
| WED | 01 | 02 | 03 | 04 | 05 | 06 | 07 | 08 | 09 | 10 | 11 | 12 | |
| THU | 01 | 02 | 03 | 04 | 05 | 06 | 07 | 08 | 09 | 10 | 11 | 12 | |
| FRI | 01 | 02 | 03 | 04 | 05 | 06 | 07 | 08 | 09 | 10 | 11 | 12 | |
| SAT | 01 | 02 | 03 | 04 | 05 | 06 | 07 | 08 | 09 | 10 | 11 | 12 | |
| SUN | 01 | 02 | 03 | 04 | 05 | 06 | 07 | 08 | 09 | 10 | 11 | 12 | |

# DEPRESSION Tracker

**Document the days when you experienced depression.**

DEPRESSION LEVELS (1-MILD, 10 SEVERE)                                    NOTES

| | | | | | | | | | | | | | |
|---|---|---|---|---|---|---|---|---|---|---|---|---|---|
| MON | 01 | 02 | 03 | 04 | 05 | 06 | 07 | 08 | 09 | 10 | 11 | 12 | |
| TUE | 01 | 02 | 03 | 04 | 05 | 06 | 07 | 08 | 09 | 10 | 11 | 12 | |
| WED | 01 | 02 | 03 | 04 | 05 | 06 | 07 | 08 | 09 | 10 | 11 | 12 | |
| THU | 01 | 02 | 03 | 04 | 05 | 06 | 07 | 08 | 09 | 10 | 11 | 12 | |
| FRI | 01 | 02 | 03 | 04 | 05 | 06 | 07 | 08 | 09 | 10 | 11 | 12 | |
| SAT | 01 | 02 | 03 | 04 | 05 | 06 | 07 | 08 | 09 | 10 | 11 | 12 | |
| SUN | 01 | 02 | 03 | 04 | 05 | 06 | 07 | 08 | 09 | 10 | 11 | 12 | |
| MON | 01 | 02 | 03 | 04 | 05 | 06 | 07 | 08 | 09 | 10 | 11 | 12 | |
| TUE | 01 | 02 | 03 | 04 | 05 | 06 | 07 | 08 | 09 | 10 | 11 | 12 | |
| WED | 01 | 02 | 03 | 04 | 05 | 06 | 07 | 08 | 09 | 10 | 11 | 12 | |
| THU | 01 | 02 | 03 | 04 | 05 | 06 | 07 | 08 | 09 | 10 | 11 | 12 | |
| FRI | 01 | 02 | 03 | 04 | 05 | 06 | 07 | 08 | 09 | 10 | 11 | 12 | |
| SAT | 01 | 02 | 03 | 04 | 05 | 06 | 07 | 08 | 09 | 10 | 11 | 12 | |
| SUN | 01 | 02 | 03 | 04 | 05 | 06 | 07 | 08 | 09 | 10 | 11 | 12 | |
| MON | 01 | 02 | 03 | 04 | 05 | 06 | 07 | 08 | 09 | 10 | 11 | 12 | |
| TUE | 01 | 02 | 03 | 04 | 05 | 06 | 07 | 08 | 09 | 10 | 11 | 12 | |
| WED | 01 | 02 | 03 | 04 | 05 | 06 | 07 | 08 | 09 | 10 | 11 | 12 | |
| THU | 01 | 02 | 03 | 04 | 05 | 06 | 07 | 08 | 09 | 10 | 11 | 12 | |
| FRI | 01 | 02 | 03 | 04 | 05 | 06 | 07 | 08 | 09 | 10 | 11 | 12 | |
| SAT | 01 | 02 | 03 | 04 | 05 | 06 | 07 | 08 | 09 | 10 | 11 | 12 | |
| SUN | 01 | 02 | 03 | 04 | 05 | 06 | 07 | 08 | 09 | 10 | 11 | 12 | |
| MON | 01 | 02 | 03 | 04 | 05 | 06 | 07 | 08 | 09 | 10 | 11 | 12 | |
| TUE | 01 | 02 | 03 | 04 | 05 | 06 | 07 | 08 | 09 | 10 | 11 | 12 | |
| WED | 01 | 02 | 03 | 04 | 05 | 06 | 07 | 08 | 09 | 10 | 11 | 12 | |
| THU | 01 | 02 | 03 | 04 | 05 | 06 | 07 | 08 | 09 | 10 | 11 | 12 | |
| FRI | 01 | 02 | 03 | 04 | 05 | 06 | 07 | 08 | 09 | 10 | 11 | 12 | |
| SAT | 01 | 02 | 03 | 04 | 05 | 06 | 07 | 08 | 09 | 10 | 11 | 12 | |
| SUN | 01 | 02 | 03 | 04 | 05 | 06 | 07 | 08 | 09 | 10 | 11 | 12 | |

# DAILY Reflection

DATE: _____

## HOW I FEEL TODAY

## MY GREATEST CHALLENGE

## MOOD TRACKER:

MORNING:

EVENING:

I FELT HAPPY WHEN:

I FELT EXCITED WHEN:

I FELT ENERGIZED WHEN:

## Today's Highlights

## What I'm Grateful For Today

# DAILY *Reflection*

HOW I FEEL TODAY

MY GREATEST CHALLENGE

MOOD TRACKER:

MORNING:

EVENING:

I FELT HAPPY WHEN:

I FELT EXCITED WHEN:

I FELT ENERGIZED WHEN:

*Today's Highlights*

*What I'm Grateful For Today*

# DAILY Reflection

DATE: _____

## HOW I FEEL TODAY

## MY GREATEST CHALLENGE

## MOOD TRACKER:

MORNING:

EVENING:

I FELT HAPPY WHEN:

I FELT EXCITED WHEN:

I FELT ENERGIZED WHEN:

## Today's Highlights

## What I'm Grateful For Today

# DAILY Reflection

DATE: _____

HOW I FEEL TODAY

MY GREATEST CHALLENGE

MOOD TRACKER:

MORNING:

EVENING:

I FELT HAPPY WHEN:

I FELT EXCITED WHEN:

I FELT ENERGIZED WHEN:

## Today's Highlights

## What I'm Grateful For Today

# DAILY Reflection

DATE: _____

## HOW I FEEL TODAY

## MY GREATEST CHALLENGE

## MOOD TRACKER:

MORNING:

EVENING:

I FELT HAPPY WHEN:

I FELT EXCITED WHEN:

I FELT ENERGIZED WHEN:

## Today's Highlights

## What I'm Grateful For Today

# DAILY Reflection

DATE: _____

HOW I FEEL TODAY

MY GREATEST CHALLENGE

MOOD TRACKER:

MORNING:                                        EVENING:

I FELT HAPPY WHEN:        I FELT EXCITED WHEN:        I FELT ENERGIZED WHEN:

## Today's Highlights

## What I'm Grateful For Today

# DAILY Reflection

DATE: _____

HOW I FEEL TODAY

MY GREATEST CHALLENGE

MOOD TRACKER:

MORNING:

EVENING:

I FELT HAPPY WHEN:

I FELT EXCITED WHEN:

I FELT ENERGIZED WHEN:

## Today's Highlights

## What I'm Grateful For Today

# POST THERAPY Chart

## SUMMARY/OVERVIEW OF THERAPY SESSION

WHAT WE DISCUSSED

HOW IT MADE ME FEEL

WHAT I LEARNED

WHAT I WANT TO DISCUSS NEXT

**Rate your session to keep track of progress.**

SESSION SCORE

# WEEKLY Assessment

WEEK OF:

| | SLEEP | MOOD | POSITIVES | NEGATIVES |
|---|---|---|---|---|
| MONDAY | | | | |
| TUESDAY | | | | |
| WEDNESDAY | | | | |
| THURSDAY | | | | |
| FRIDAY | | | | |
| SATURADY | | | | |
| SUNDAY | | | | |

# DAILY Reflection

HOW I FEEL TODAY

MY GREATEST CHALLENGE

MOOD TRACKER:

MORNING:

EVENING:

I FELT HAPPY WHEN:

I FELT EXCITED WHEN

I FELT ENERGIZED WHEN

## Today's Highlights

## What I'm Grateful For Today

# DAILY Reflection

DATE: _____

## HOW I FEEL TODAY

## MY GREATEST CHALLENGE

## MOOD TRACKER:

MORNING:

EVENING:

I FELT HAPPY WHEN:

I FELT EXCITED WHEN:

I FELT ENERGIZED WHEN:

## Today's Highlights

## What I'm Grateful For Today

# DAILY Reflection

HOW I FEEL TODAY

MY GREATEST CHALLENGE

MOOD TRACKER:

MORNING:

EVENING:

I FELT HAPPY WHEN:

I FELT EXCITED WHEN:

I FELT ENERGIZED WHEN:

## Today's Highlights

## What I'm Grateful For Today

# DAILY Reflection

DATE: _____

HOW I FEEL TODAY

MY GREATEST CHALLENGE

MOOD TRACKER:

MORNING:

EVENING:

I FELT HAPPY WHEN:

I FELT EXCITED WHEN:

I FELT ENERGIZED WHEN:

## Today's Highlights

## What I'm Grateful For Today

# DAILY Reflection

DATE: _____

HOW I FEEL TODAY

MY GREATEST CHALLENGE

MOOD TRACKER:

MORNING:

EVENING:

I FELT HAPPY WHEN:

I FELT EXCITED WHEN:

I FELT ENERGIZED WHEN:

Today's Highlights

What I'm Grateful For Today

# DAILY Reflection

DATE: _____

HOW I FEEL TODAY

MY GREATEST CHALLENGE

MOOD TRACKER:

MORNING:

EVENING:

I FELT HAPPY WHEN:

I FELT EXCITED WHEN:

I FELT ENERGIZED WHEN:

## Today's Highlights

## What I'm Grateful For Today

# DAILY *Reflection*

DATE: _____

HOW I FEEL TODAY

MY GREATEST CHALLENGE

MOOD TRACKER:

MORNING:

EVENING:

I FELT HAPPY WHEN:

I FELT EXCITED WHEN:

I FELT ENERGIZED WHEN:

*Today's Highlights*

*What I'm Grateful For Today*

# POST THERAPY *Chart*

DATE:

## SUMMARY/OVERVIEW OF THERAPY SESSION

## WHAT WE DISCUSSED

## HOW IT MADE ME FEEL

## WHAT I LEARNED

## WHAT I WANT TO DISCUSS NEXT

**Rate your session to keep track of progress.**

SESSION SCORE

# WEEKLY Assessment

WEEK OF:

| | SLEEP | MOOD | POSITIVES | NEGATIVES |
|---|---|---|---|---|
| MONDAY | | | | |
| TUESDAY | | | | |
| WEDNESDAY | | | | |
| THURSDAY | | | | |
| FRIDAY | | | | |
| SATURADY | | | | |
| SUNDAY | | | | |

# DAILY *Reflection*

DATE: _____

### HOW I FEEL TODAY

### MY GREATEST CHALLENGE

### MOOD TRACKER:

MORNING:

EVENING:

I FELT HAPPY WHEN:

I FELT EXCITED WHEN:

I FELT ENERGIZED WHEN:

## Today's Highlights

## What I'm Grateful For Today

# DAILY *Reflection*

DATE: _____

HOW I FEEL TODAY                    MY GREATEST CHALLENGE

MOOD TRACKER:

MORNING:                            EVENING:

I FELT HAPPY WHEN:        I FELT EXCITED WHEN:        I FELT ENERGIZED WHEN:

## Today's Highlights

## What I'm Grateful For Today

# DAILY Reflection

DATE: _____

## HOW I FEEL TODAY

## MY GREATEST CHALLENGE

## MOOD TRACKER:

MORNING:

EVENING:

I FELT HAPPY WHEN:

I FELT EXCITED WHEN:

I FELT ENERGIZED WHEN:

## Today's Highlights

## What I'm Grateful For Today

# DAILY Reflection

HOW I FEEL TODAY                    MY GREATEST CHALLENGE

MOOD TRACKER:

MORNING:                                        EVENING:

I FELT HAPPY WHEN:        I FELT EXCITED WHEN        I FELT ENERGIZED WHEN

## Today's Highlights

## What I'm Grateful For Today

# DAILY Reflection

DATE: _____

**HOW I FEEL TODAY**

**MY GREATEST CHALLENGE**

**MOOD TRACKER:**

MORNING:

EVENING:

I FELT HAPPY WHEN:

I FELT EXCITED WHEN:

I FELT ENERGIZED WHEN:

## Today's Highlights

## What I'm Grateful For Today

# DAILY Reflection

DATE: _____

HOW I FEEL TODAY                    MY GREATEST CHALLENGE

MOOD TRACKER:

MORNING:                                    EVENING:

I FELT HAPPY WHEN:        I FELT EXCITED WHEN:        I FELT ENERGIZED WHEN:

## Today's Highlights

## What I'm Grateful For Today

# DAILY Reflection

## HOW I FEEL TODAY

## MY GREATEST CHALLENGE

## MOOD TRACKER:

MORNING:

EVENING:

I FELT HAPPY WHEN:

I FELT EXCITED WHEN:

I FELT ENERGIZED WHEN:

## Today's Highlights

## What I'm Grateful For Today

# WEEKLY Assessment

WEEK OF:

| | SLEEP | MOOD | POSITIVES | NEGATIVES |
|---|---|---|---|---|
| MONDAY | | | | |
| TUESDAY | | | | |
| WEDNESDAY | | | | |
| THURSDAY | | | | |
| FRIDAY | | | | |
| SATURADAY | | | | |
| SUNDAY | | | | |

# POST THERAPY *Chart*

DATE:

## SUMMARY/OVERVIEW OF THERAPY SESSION

## WHAT WE DISCUSSED

## HOW IT MADE ME FEEL

## WHAT I LEARNED

## WHAT I WANT TO DISCUSS NEXT

**Rate your session to keep track of progress.**

SESSION SCORE

# DAILY Reflection

DATE: _____

HOW I FEEL TODAY

MY GREATEST CHALLENGE

MOOD TRACKER:

MORNING:

EVENING:

I FELT HAPPY WHEN:

I FELT EXCITED WHEN:

I FELT ENERGIZED WHEN:

## Today's Highlights

## What I'm Grateful For Today

# DAILY Reflection

DATE: _____

HOW I FEEL TODAY

MY GREATEST CHALLENGE

MOOD TRACKER:

MORNING:

EVENING:

I FELT HAPPY WHEN:

I FELT EXCITED WHEN:

I FELT ENERGIZED WHEN:

## Today's Highlights

## What I'm Grateful For Today

# DAILY Reflection

DATE: _____

HOW I FEEL TODAY                    MY GREATEST CHALLENGE

MOOD TRACKER:

MORNING:                                    EVENING:

I FELT HAPPY WHEN          I FELT EXCITED WHEN          I FELT ENERGIZED WHEN:

Today's Highlights

What I'm Grateful For Today

# DAILY Reflection

DATE: _____

## HOW I FEEL TODAY

## MY GREATEST CHALLENGE

## MOOD TRACKER:

MORNING:

EVENING:

I FELT HAPPY WHEN:

I FELT EXCITED WHEN:

I FELT ENERGIZED WHEN:

## Today's Highlights

## What I'm Grateful For Today

# DAILY Reflection

DATE: _____

HOW I FEEL TODAY

MY GREATEST CHALLENGE

MOOD TRACKER:

MORNING:

EVENING:

I FELT HAPPY WHEN:

I FELT EXCITED WHEN:

I FELT ENERGIZED WHEN:

## Today's Highlights

## What I'm Grateful For Today

# DAILY Reflection

DATE: _____

### HOW I FEEL TODAY

### MY GREATEST CHALLENGE

### MOOD TRACKER:

MORNING:

EVENING:

I FELT HAPPY WHEN:

I FELT EXCITED WHEN:

I FELT ENERGIZED WHEN:

## Today's Highlights

## What I'm Grateful For Today

# DAILY *Reflection*

HOW I FEEL TODAY

MY GREATEST CHALLENGE

MOOD TRACKER:

MORNING:

EVENING:

I FELT HAPPY WHEN:

I FELT EXCITED WHEN:

I FELT ENERGIZED WHEN:

## Today's Highlights

## What I'm Grateful For Today

# POST THERAPY *Chart*

## SUMMARY/OVERVIEW OF THERAPY SESSION

### WHAT WE DISCUSSED

### HOW IT MADE ME FEEL

### WHAT I LEARNED

### WHAT I WANT TO DISCUSS NEXT

**Rate your session to keep track of progress.**

SESSION SCORE

# WEEKLY Assessment

WEEK OF:

| | SLEEP | MOOD | POSITIVES | NEGATIVES |
|---|---|---|---|---|
| MONDAY | | | | |
| TUESDAY | | | | |
| WEDNESDAY | | | | |
| THURSDAY | | | | |
| FRIDAY | | | | |
| SATURADY | | | | |
| SUNDAY | | | | |

# DAILY Reflection

DATE: _____

HOW I FEEL TODAY

MY GREATEST CHALLENGE

MOOD TRACKER:

MORNING:

EVENING:

I FELT HAPPY WHEN:

I FELT EXCITED WHEN:

I FELT ENERGIZED WHEN:

## Today's Highlights

## What I'm Grateful For Today

# DAILY Reflection

HOW I FEEL TODAY

MY GREATEST CHALLENGE

MOOD TRACKER:

MORNING:

EVENING:

I FELT HAPPY WHEN:

I FELT EXCITED WHEN:

I FELT ENERGIZED WHEN:

## Today's Highlights

## What I'm Grateful For Today

# DAILY Reflection

DATE: _____

## HOW I FEEL TODAY

## MY GREATEST CHALLENGE

## MOOD TRACKER:

MORNING:

EVENING:

I FELT HAPPY WHEN:

I FELT EXCITED WHEN:

I FELT ENERGIZED WHEN:

### Today's Highlights

### What I'm Grateful For Today

# ANXIETY Levels

Use the chart below to rate your level of anxiety when facing various situations by coloring the boxes:

**SITUATION:** Meeting someone new

**ANXIETY LEVEL:**

**DO YOU:**       Face this fear          Avoid this situation


**SITUATION:** Going shopping or to the grocery store

**ANXIETY LEVEL:**

**DO YOU:**       Face this fear          Avoid this situation


**SITUATION:** Stating your opinion when potentially controversial or opposing

**ANXIETY LEVEL:**

**DO YOU:**       Face this fear          Avoid this situation


**SITUATION:** Standing up for yourself when treated unfairly or poorly

**ANXIETY LEVEL:**

**DO YOU:**       Face this fear          Avoid this situation


**SITUATION:** Spending time alone with friends and/or family

**ANXIETY LEVEL:**

**DO YOU:**       Face this fear          Avoid this situation


**SITUATION:** Being watched/observed when doing something/completing a task or activity

**ANXIETY LEVEL:**

**DO YOU:**       Face this fear          Avoid this situation

# ANXIETY Debrief

**Describe a situation where you felt anxious:**

**What were the physical symptoms you experienced?**

**Did you face the situation or remove yourself from it?**

**How did you cope with this anxiety?**
**Do you believe your thoughts and reactions were rational?**

# MOOD Chart

Use the wheel below to document your moods every month.
Use **3 different colors** to represent
positive, negative or neutral emotions.

POSITIVE     NEGATIVE     NEUTRAL

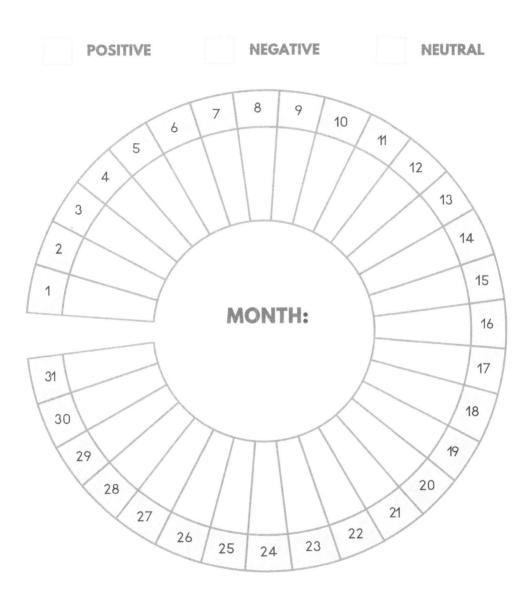

MONTH:

# TRIGGER *Tracker*

**Keep track of experiences that generate
negative thoughts and emotions.**

| DATE | INCIDENT | REACTION |
|------|----------|----------|
|      |          |          |
|      |          |          |
|      |          |          |
|      |          |          |
|      |          |          |
|      |          |          |
|      |          |          |
|      |          |          |
|      |          |          |

# SLEEP Tracker

**Sleep plays a major factor in our ability to cope
with anxiety and depression.
Keep track of your sleep pattern in order to determine
how the amount of rest may be affecting your mental health.**

| DAY | HOURS SLEPT | QUALITY OF SLEEP | THOUGHTS |
|-----|-------------|------------------|----------|
| 1 | | | |
| 2 | | | |
| 3 | | | |
| 4 | | | |
| 5 | | | |
| 6 | | | |
| 7 | | | |
| 8 | | | |
| 9 | | | |
| 10 | | | |
| 11 | | | |
| 12 | | | |
| 13 | | | |
| 14 | | | |
| 15 | | | |
| 16 | | | |
| 17 | | | |
| 18 | | | |
| 19 | | | |
| 20 | | | |
| 21 | | | |
| 22 | | | |
| 23 | | | |
| 24 | | | |
| 25 | | | |
| 26 | | | |
| 27 | | | |
| 28 | | | |
| 29 | | | |
| 30 | | | |
| 31 | | | |

# GRATEFUL Heart

| DAY | TODAY I AM GRATEFUL FOR: |
|-----|--------------------------|
| 1 | |
| 2 | |
| 3 | |
| 4 | |
| 5 | |
| 6 | |
| 7 | |
| 8 | |
| 9 | |
| 10 | |
| 11 | |
| 12 | |
| 13 | |
| 14 | |
| 15 | |
| 16 | |
| 17 | |
| 18 | |
| 19 | |
| 20 | |
| 21 | |
| 22 | |
| 23 | |
| 24 | |
| 25 | |
| 26 | |
| 27 | |
| 28 | |
| 29 | |
| 30 | |
| 31 | |

# SELF CARE Tracker

Self care is an important step in managing anxiety and depression.
It helps us recharge, reset and nurtures our mind and soul.
Focus on incorporating one self-care activity into your daily life.

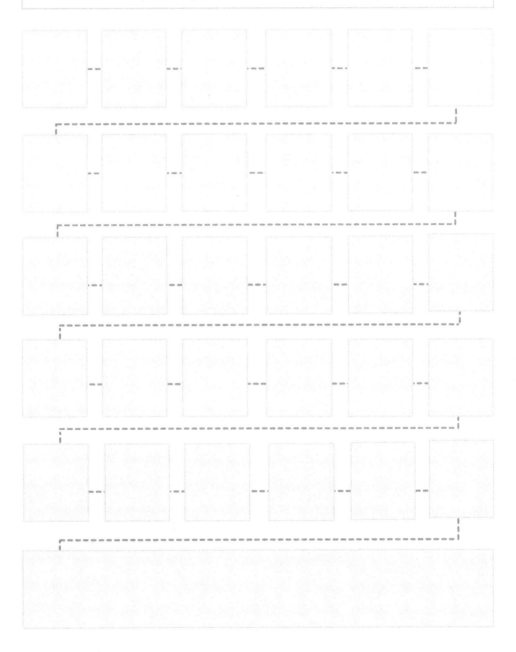

# THOUGHT Log

**Keep track of negative thoughts so you can
learn how to control irrational responses and triggers.**

| DATE | INCIDENT | INITIAL REACTION | RATIONAL REACTION |
|------|----------|------------------|-------------------|
|      |          |                  |                   |
|      |          |                  |                   |
|      |          |                  |                   |
|      |          |                  |                   |
|      |          |                  |                   |
|      |          |                  |                   |
|      |          |                  |                   |
|      |          |                  |                   |
|      |          |                  |                   |
|      |          |                  |                   |

# HAPPINESS Tracker

**Keep track of how often you feel happy and calm
and what you did to minimize negative responses.**

DATE:                                    DATE:

HAPPINESS RATING: ☆☆☆☆☆    HAPPINESS RATING: ☆☆☆☆☆

DATE:                                    DATE:

HAPPINESS RATING: ☆☆☆☆☆    HAPPINESS RATING: ☆☆☆☆☆

DATE:                                    DATE:

HAPPINESS RATING: ☆☆☆☆☆    HAPPINESS RATING: ☆☆☆☆☆

# PERSONAL *Wins*

It's important to celebrate both minor and major wins
when it comes to your mental health
and the coping  strategies you've learned along the way.
You've come a long way!

## 2 RECENT WINS

|  |  |
|---|---|
|  |  |

## TOP 3 MILESTONES

| 1 |  |
|---|---|
| 2 |  |
| 3 |  |

## 3 THINGS I'VE LEARNED ABOUT MYSELF OVER THE LAST YEAR

|  |  |  |
|---|---|---|
|  |  |  |

| PERSONAL REFLECTIONS | HOW I'VE LEARNED TO COPE WITH EMOTIONS |
|---|---|
|  |  |
|  |  |
|  |  |
|  |  |
|  |  |

## NOTES

|  |
|---|
|  |
|  |
|  |
|  |
|  |
|  |
|  |

# PERSONAL Rewards

**Make sure to reward yourself for accomplishments throughout your journey.**
**Whether it's a visit to your favorite restaurant, a bubble bath, or an evening with friends, it's important to celebrate your progress every step of the way.**

### IDEAS FOR PERSONAL REWARDS

| | |
|---|---|
| 1 | 2 |
| 3 | 4 |
| 5 | 6 |

| HOW I FELT BEFORE | HOW I REWARDED MYSELF | HOW I FELT AFTERWARD |
|---|---|---|
| | | |
| | | |
| | | |
| | | |
| | | |
| | | |
| | | |

| NOTES | PERSONAL REFLECTIONS/THOUGHTS |
|---|---|
| | |

# ANXIETY Tracker

**Document the days when you experienced anxiety.**

ANXIETY LEVELS (1-MILD, 10 SEVERE)                    NOTES

| | | | | | | | | | | | | |
|---|---|---|---|---|---|---|---|---|---|---|---|---|
| MON | 01 | 02 | 03 | 04 | 05 | 06 | 07 | 08 | 09 | 10 | 11 | 12 |
| TUE | 01 | 02 | 03 | 04 | 05 | 06 | 07 | 08 | 09 | 10 | 11 | 12 |
| WED | 01 | 02 | 03 | 04 | 05 | 06 | 07 | 08 | 09 | 10 | 11 | 12 |
| THU | 01 | 02 | 03 | 04 | 05 | 06 | 07 | 08 | 09 | 10 | 11 | 12 |
| FRI | 01 | 02 | 03 | 04 | 05 | 06 | 07 | 08 | 09 | 10 | 11 | 12 |
| SAT | 01 | 02 | 03 | 04 | 05 | 06 | 07 | 08 | 09 | 10 | 11 | 12 |
| SUN | 01 | 02 | 03 | 04 | 05 | 06 | 07 | 08 | 09 | 10 | 11 | 12 |
| MON | 01 | 02 | 03 | 04 | 05 | 06 | 07 | 08 | 09 | 10 | 11 | 12 |
| TUE | 01 | 02 | 03 | 04 | 05 | 06 | 07 | 08 | 09 | 10 | 11 | 12 |
| WED | 01 | 02 | 03 | 04 | 05 | 06 | 07 | 08 | 09 | 10 | 11 | 12 |
| THU | 01 | 02 | 03 | 04 | 05 | 06 | 07 | 08 | 09 | 10 | 11 | 12 |
| FRI | 01 | 02 | 03 | 04 | 05 | 06 | 07 | 08 | 09 | 10 | 11 | 12 |
| SAT | 01 | 02 | 03 | 04 | 05 | 06 | 07 | 08 | 09 | 10 | 11 | 12 |
| SUN | 01 | 02 | 03 | 04 | 05 | 06 | 07 | 08 | 09 | 10 | 11 | 12 |
| MON | 01 | 02 | 03 | 04 | 05 | 06 | 07 | 08 | 09 | 10 | 11 | 12 |
| TUE | 01 | 02 | 03 | 04 | 05 | 06 | 07 | 08 | 09 | 10 | 11 | 12 |
| WED | 01 | 02 | 03 | 04 | 05 | 06 | 07 | 08 | 09 | 10 | 11 | 12 |
| THU | 01 | 02 | 03 | 04 | 05 | 06 | 07 | 08 | 09 | 10 | 11 | 12 |
| FRI | 01 | 02 | 03 | 04 | 05 | 06 | 07 | 08 | 09 | 10 | 11 | 12 |
| SAT | 01 | 02 | 03 | 04 | 05 | 06 | 07 | 08 | 09 | 10 | 11 | 12 |
| SUN | 01 | 02 | 03 | 04 | 05 | 06 | 07 | 08 | 09 | 10 | 11 | 12 |
| MON | 01 | 02 | 03 | 04 | 05 | 06 | 07 | 08 | 09 | 10 | 11 | 12 |
| TUE | 01 | 02 | 03 | 04 | 05 | 06 | 07 | 08 | 09 | 10 | 11 | 12 |
| WED | 01 | 02 | 03 | 04 | 05 | 06 | 07 | 08 | 09 | 10 | 11 | 12 |
| THU | 01 | 02 | 03 | 04 | 05 | 06 | 07 | 08 | 09 | 10 | 11 | 12 |
| FRI | 01 | 02 | 03 | 04 | 05 | 06 | 07 | 08 | 09 | 10 | 11 | 12 |
| SAT | 01 | 02 | 03 | 04 | 05 | 06 | 07 | 08 | 09 | 10 | 11 | 12 |
| SUN | 01 | 02 | 03 | 04 | 05 | 06 | 07 | 08 | 09 | 10 | 11 | 12 |

# DEPRESSION *Tracker*

**Document the days when you experienced depression.**

DEPRESSION LEVELS (1-MILD, 10 SEVERE)                                   NOTES

| | | | | | | | | | | | | | NOTES |
|---|---|---|---|---|---|---|---|---|---|---|---|---|---|
| MON | 01 | 02 | 03 | 04 | 05 | 06 | 07 | 08 | 09 | 10 | 11 | 12 | |
| TUE | 01 | 02 | 03 | 04 | 05 | 06 | 07 | 08 | 09 | 10 | 11 | 12 | |
| WED | 01 | 02 | 03 | 04 | 05 | 06 | 07 | 08 | 09 | 10 | 11 | 12 | |
| THU | 01 | 02 | 03 | 04 | 05 | 06 | 07 | 08 | 09 | 10 | 11 | 12 | |
| FRI | 01 | 02 | 03 | 04 | 05 | 06 | 07 | 08 | 09 | 10 | 11 | 12 | |
| SAT | 01 | 02 | 03 | 04 | 05 | 06 | 07 | 08 | 09 | 10 | 11 | 12 | |
| SUN | 01 | 02 | 03 | 04 | 05 | 06 | 07 | 08 | 09 | 10 | 11 | 12 | |
| MON | 01 | 02 | 03 | 04 | 05 | 06 | 07 | 08 | 09 | 10 | 11 | 12 | |
| TUE | 01 | 02 | 03 | 04 | 05 | 06 | 07 | 08 | 09 | 10 | 11 | 12 | |
| WED | 01 | 02 | 03 | 04 | 05 | 06 | 07 | 08 | 09 | 10 | 11 | 12 | |
| THU | 01 | 02 | 03 | 04 | 05 | 06 | 07 | 08 | 09 | 10 | 11 | 12 | |
| FRI | 01 | 02 | 03 | 04 | 05 | 06 | 07 | 08 | 09 | 10 | 11 | 12 | |
| SAT | 01 | 02 | 03 | 04 | 05 | 06 | 07 | 08 | 09 | 10 | 11 | 12 | |
| SUN | 01 | 02 | 03 | 04 | 05 | 06 | 07 | 08 | 09 | 10 | 11 | 12 | |
| MON | 01 | 02 | 03 | 04 | 05 | 06 | 07 | 08 | 09 | 10 | 11 | 12 | |
| TUE | 01 | 02 | 03 | 04 | 05 | 06 | 07 | 08 | 09 | 10 | 11 | 12 | |
| WED | 01 | 02 | 03 | 04 | 05 | 06 | 07 | 08 | 09 | 10 | 11 | 12 | |
| THU | 01 | 02 | 03 | 04 | 05 | 06 | 07 | 08 | 09 | 10 | 11 | 12 | |
| FRI | 01 | 02 | 03 | 04 | 05 | 06 | 07 | 08 | 09 | 10 | 11 | 12 | |
| SAT | 01 | 02 | 03 | 04 | 05 | 06 | 07 | 08 | 09 | 10 | 11 | 12 | |
| SUN | 01 | 02 | 03 | 04 | 05 | 06 | 07 | 08 | 09 | 10 | 11 | 12 | |
| MON | 01 | 02 | 03 | 04 | 05 | 06 | 07 | 08 | 09 | 10 | 11 | 12 | |
| TUE | 01 | 02 | 03 | 04 | 05 | 06 | 07 | 08 | 09 | 10 | 11 | 12 | |
| WED | 01 | 02 | 03 | 04 | 05 | 06 | 07 | 08 | 09 | 10 | 11 | 12 | |
| THU | 01 | 02 | 03 | 04 | 05 | 06 | 07 | 08 | 09 | 10 | 11 | 12 | |
| FRI | 01 | 02 | 03 | 04 | 05 | 06 | 07 | 08 | 09 | 10 | 11 | 12 | |
| SAT | 01 | 02 | 03 | 04 | 05 | 06 | 07 | 08 | 09 | 10 | 11 | 12 | |
| SUN | 01 | 02 | 03 | 04 | 05 | 06 | 07 | 08 | 09 | 10 | 11 | 12 | |

# DAILY Reflection

DATE: _____

### HOW I FEEL TODAY

### MY GREATEST CHALLENGE

### MOOD TRACKER:

MORNING:

EVENING:

I FELT HAPPY WHEN:

I FELT EXCITED WHEN:

I FELT ENERGIZED WHEN:

## Today's Highlights

## What I'm Grateful For Today

# DAILY *Reflection*

DATE: _____

HOW I FEEL TODAY

MY GREATEST CHALLENGE

MOOD TRACKER:

MORNING:

EVENING:

I FELT HAPPY WHEN

I FELT EXCITED WHEN:

I FELT ENERGIZED WHEN:

## Today's Highlights

## What I'm Grateful For Today

# DAILY Reflection

DATE: _____

### HOW I FEEL TODAY

### MY GREATEST CHALLENGE

### MOOD TRACKER:

MORNING:

EVENING:

I FELT HAPPY WHEN:

I FELT EXCITED WHEN:

I FELT ENERGIZED WHEN:

## Today's Highlights

## What I'm Grateful For Today

# DAILY Reflection

DATE: _____

HOW I FEEL TODAY

MY GREATEST CHALLENGE

MOOD TRACKER:

MORNING:

EVENING:

I FELT HAPPY WHEN:

I FELT EXCITED WHEN:

I FELT ENERGIZED WHEN:

## Today's Highlights

## What I'm Grateful For Today

# DAILY Reflection

DATE: _____

HOW I FEEL TODAY

MY GREATEST CHALLENGE

MOOD TRACKER:

MORNING:

EVENING:

I FELT HAPPY WHEN:

I FELT EXCITED WHEN:

I FELT ENERGIZED WHEN:

## Today's Highlights

## What I'm Grateful For Today

# DAILY Reflection

DATE: _____

HOW I FEEL TODAY

MY GREATEST CHALLENGE

MOOD TRACKER:

MORNING:

EVENING:

I FELT HAPPY WHEN:

I FELT EXCITED WHEN

I FELT ENERGIZED WHEN

## Today's Highlights

## What I'm Grateful For Today

# DAILY Reflection

DATE: _____

## HOW I FEEL TODAY

## MY GREATEST CHALLENGE

## MOOD TRACKER:

MORNING:

EVENING:

I FELT HAPPY WHEN:

I FELT EXCITED WHEN:

I FELT ENERGIZED WHEN:

## Today's Highlights

## What I'm Grateful For Today

# WEEKLY Assessment

WEEK OF:

| | SLEEP | MOOD | POSITIVES | NEGATIVES |
|---|---|---|---|---|
| MONDAY | | | | |
| TUESDAY | | | | |
| WEDNESDAY | | | | |
| THURSDAY | | | | |
| FRIDAY | | | | |
| SATURADY | | | | |
| SUNDAY | | | | |

# POST THERAPY *Chart*

DATE:

## SUMMARY/OVERVIEW OF THERAPY SESSION

### WHAT WE DISCUSSED

### HOW IT MADE ME FEEL

### WHAT I LEARNED

### WHAT I WANT TO DISCUSS NEXT

Rate your session to keep track of progress.

SESSION SCORE

# DAILY *Reflection*

DATE: _____

HOW I FEEL TODAY                    MY GREATEST CHALLENGE

MOOD TRACKER:

MORNING:                              EVENING:

I FELT HAPPY WHEN:        I FELT EXCITED WHEN:        I FELT ENERGIZED WHEN:

## Today's Highlights

## What I'm Grateful For Today

# DAILY *Reflection*

DATE: _____

### HOW I FEEL TODAY

### MY GREATEST CHALLENGE

### MOOD TRACKER:

MORNING:

EVENING:

I FELT HAPPY WHEN:

I FELT EXCITED WHEN:

I FELT ENERGIZED WHEN:

## Today's Highlights

## What I'm Grateful For Today

# DAILY *Reflection*

HOW I FEEL TODAY                    MY GREATEST CHALLENGE

MOOD TRACKER:

MORNING:                              EVENING:

I FELT HAPPY WHEN:        I FELT EXCITED WHEN:        I FELT ENERGIZED WHEN:

## Today's Highlights

## What I'm Grateful For Today

# DAILY Reflection

DATE: _____

## HOW I FEEL TODAY

## MY GREATEST CHALLENGE

## MOOD TRACKER:

MORNING:

EVENING:

I FELT HAPPY WHEN:

I FELT EXCITED WHEN:

I FELT ENERGIZED WHEN:

## Today's Highlights

## What I'm Grateful For Today

# DAILY Reflection

DATE: _____

HOW I FEEL TODAY

MY GREATEST CHALLENGE

MOOD TRACKER:

MORNING:

EVENING:

I FELT HAPPY WHEN:

I FELT EXCITED WHEN:

I FELT ENERGIZED WHEN:

## Today's Highlights

## What I'm Grateful For Today

# DAILY Reflection

DATE: _____

## HOW I FEEL TODAY

## MY GREATEST CHALLENGE

## MOOD TRACKER:

MORNING:

EVENING:

I FELT HAPPY WHEN:

I FELT EXCITED WHEN:

I FELT ENERGIZED WHEN:

## Today's Highlights

## What I'm Grateful For Today

# DAILY Reflection

DATE: _____

HOW I FEEL TODAY

MY GREATEST CHALLENGE

MOOD TRACKER:

MORNING:

EVENING:

I FELT HAPPY WHEN:

I FELT EXCITED WHEN:

I FELT ENERGIZED WHEN:

## Today's Highlights

## What I'm Grateful For Today

# POST THERAPY Chart

DATE:

## SUMMARY/OVERVIEW OF THERAPY SESSION

## WHAT WE DISCUSSED

## HOW IT MADE ME FEEL

## WHAT I LEARNED

## WHAT I WANT TO DISCUSS NEXT

**Rate your session to keep track of progress.**

SESSION SCORE

# WEEKLY Assessment

WEEK OF:

| | SLEEP | MOOD | POSITIVES | NEGATIVES |
|---|---|---|---|---|
| MONDAY | | | | |
| TUESDAY | | | | |
| WEDNESDAY | | | | |
| THURSDAY | | | | |
| FRIDAY | | | | |
| SATURADY | | | | |
| SUNDAY | | | | |

# DAILY Reflection

DATE: _____

## HOW I FEEL TODAY

## MY GREATEST CHALLENGE

## MOOD TRACKER:

MORNING:

EVENING:

I FELT HAPPY WHEN:

I FELT EXCITED WHEN:

I FELT ENERGIZED WHEN:

## Today's Highlights

## What I'm Grateful For Today

# DAILY Reflection

DATE: _____

HOW I FEEL TODAY

MY GREATEST CHALLENGE

MOOD TRACKER:

MORNING:

EVENING:

I FELT HAPPY WHEN

I FELT EXCITED WHEN

I FELT ENERGIZED WHEN

## Today's Highlights

## What I'm Grateful For Today

# DAILY Reflection

DATE: _____

## HOW I FEEL TODAY

## MY GREATEST CHALLENGE

## MOOD TRACKER:

MORNING:

EVENING:

I FELT HAPPY WHEN:

I FELT EXCITED WHEN:

I FELT ENERGIZED WHEN:

## Today's Highlights

## What I'm Grateful For Today

# DAILY Reflection

DATE: _____

HOW I FEEL TODAY

MY GREATEST CHALLENGE

MOOD TRACKER:

MORNING:

EVENING:

I FELT HAPPY WHEN:

I FELT EXCITED WHEN:

I FELT ENERGIZED WHEN:

## Today's Highlights

## What I'm Grateful For Today

# DAILY Reflection

DATE: _____

## HOW I FEEL TODAY

## MY GREATEST CHALLENGE

## MOOD TRACKER:

MORNING:

EVENING:

I FELT HAPPY WHEN:

I FELT EXCITED WHEN:

I FELT ENERGIZED WHEN:

### Today's Highlights

### What I'm Grateful For Today

# DAILY *Reflection*

DATE: _____

HOW I FEEL TODAY

MY GREATEST CHALLENGE

MOOD TRACKER:

MORNING:

EVENING:

I FELT HAPPY WHEN:

I FELT EXCITED WHEN:

I FELT ENERGIZED WHEN:

*Today's Highlights*

*What I'm Grateful For Today*

# DAILY Reflection

DATE: _____

## HOW I FEEL TODAY

## MY GREATEST CHALLENGE

## MOOD TRACKER:

MORNING:

EVENING:

I FELT HAPPY WHEN:

I FELT EXCITED WHEN:

I FELT ENERGIZED WHEN:

## Today's Highlights

## What I'm Grateful For Today

# WEEKLY Assessment

WEEK OF:

| | SLEEP | MOOD | POSITIVES | NEGATIVES |
|---|---|---|---|---|
| MONDAY | | | | |
| TUESDAY | | | | |
| WEDNESDAY | | | | |
| THURSDAY | | | | |
| FRIDAY | | | | |
| SATURADY | | | | |
| SUNDAY | | | | |

# POST THERAPY Chart

## SUMMARY/OVERVIEW OF THERAPY SESSION

### WHAT WE DISCUSSED

### HOW IT MADE ME FEEL

### WHAT I LEARNED

### WHAT I WANT TO DISCUSS NEXT

Rate your session to keep track of progress.

SESSION SCORE

# DAILY Reflection

DATE: _____

HOW I FEEL TODAY

MY GREATEST CHALLENGE

MOOD TRACKER:

MORNING:

EVENING:

I FELT HAPPY WHEN:

I FELT EXCITED WHEN:

I FELT ENERGIZED WHEN:

## Today's Highlights

## What I'm Grateful For Today

# DAILY *Reflection*

DATE: _____

HOW I FEEL TODAY

MY GREATEST CHALLENGE

MOOD TRACKER:

MORNING:

EVENING:

I FELT HAPPY WHEN:

I FELT EXCITED WHEN:

I FELT ENERGIZED WHEN:

## Today's Highlights

## What I'm Grateful For Today

# DAILY Reflection

DATE: _____

HOW I FEEL TODAY

MY GREATEST CHALLENGE

MOOD TRACKER:

MORNING:

EVENING:

I FELT HAPPY WHEN:

I FELT EXCITED WHEN:

I FELT ENERGIZED WHEN:

## Today's Highlights

## What I'm Grateful For Today

# DAILY Reflection

DATE: _____

HOW I FEEL TODAY

MY GREATEST CHALLENGE

MOOD TRACKER:

MORNING:

EVENING:

I FELT HAPPY WHEN:

I FELT EXCITED WHEN:

I FELT ENERGIZED WHEN:

## Today's Highlights

## What I'm Grateful For Today

# DAILY Reflection

DATE: _____

HOW I FEEL TODAY

MY GREATEST CHALLENGE

MOOD TRACKER:

MORNING:

EVENING:

I FELT HAPPY WHEN:

I FELT EXCITED WHEN:

I FELT ENERGIZED WHEN:

## Today's Highlights

## What I'm Grateful For Today

# DAILY *Reflection*

DATE: _____

### HOW I FEEL TODAY

### MY GREATEST CHALLENGE

### MOOD TRACKER:

MORNING.

EVENING:

I FELT HAPPY WHEN:

I FELT EXCITED WHEN:

I FELT ENERGIZED WHEN:

## Today's Highlights

## What I'm Grateful For Today

# DAILY Reflection

HOW I FEEL TODAY                    MY GREATEST CHALLENGE

MOOD TRACKER:

MORNING:                                      EVENING:

I FELT HAPPY WHEN:          I FELT EXCITED WHEN:          I FELT ENERGIZED WHEN:

## Today's Highlights

## What I'm Grateful For Today

# POST THERAPY *Chart*

DATE:

## SUMMARY/OVERVIEW OF THERAPY SESSION

## WHAT WE DISCUSSED

## HOW IT MADE ME FEEL

## WHAT I LEARNED

## WHAT I WANT TO DISCUSS NEXT

### Rate your session to keep track of progress.

SESSION SCORE

# WEEKLY Assessment

WEEK OF:

| | SLEEP | MOOD | POSITIVES | NEGATIVES |
|---|---|---|---|---|
| MONDAY | | | | |
| TUESDAY | | | | |
| WEDNESDAY | | | | |
| THURSDAY | | | | |
| FRIDAY | | | | |
| SATURADY | | | | |
| SUNDAY | | | | |

# DAILY Reflection

DATE: _____

HOW I FEEL TODAY

MY GREATEST CHALLENGE

MOOD TRACKER:

MORNING:

EVENING:

I FELT HAPPY WHEN:

I FELT EXCITED WHEN:

I FELT ENERGIZED WHEN:

## Today's Highlights

## What I'm Grateful For Today

# DAILY Reflection

DATE: _____

HOW I FEEL TODAY

MY GREATEST CHALLENGE

MOOD TRACKER:

MORNING:

EVENING:

I FELT HAPPY WHEN:

I FELT EXCITED WHEN:

I FELT ENERGIZED WHEN:

## Today's Highlights

## What I'm Grateful For Today

# DAILY Reflection

DATE: _____

### HOW I FEEL TODAY

### MY GREATEST CHALLENGE

### MOOD TRACKER:

MORNING:

EVENING:

I FELT HAPPY WHEN:

I FELT EXCITED WHEN:

I FELT ENERGIZED WHEN:

## Today's Highlights

## What I'm Grateful For Today

# ANXIETY Levels

Use the chart below to rate your level of anxiety when facing various situations by coloring the boxes:

**SITUATION:** Meeting someone new

**ANXIETY LEVEL:**

**DO YOU:**     Face this fear          Avoid this situation


**SITUATION:** Going shopping or to the grocery store

**ANXIETY LEVEL:**

**DO YOU:**     Face this fear          Avoid this situation


**SITUATION:** Stating your opinion when potentially controversial or opposing

**ANXIETY LEVEL:**

**DO YOU:**     Face this fear          Avoid this situation


**SITUATION:** Standing up for yourself when treated unfairly or poorly

**ANXIETY LEVEL:**

**DO YOU:**     Face this fear          Avoid this situation


**SITUATION:** Spending time alone with friends and/or family

**ANXIETY LEVEL:**

**DO YOU:**     Face this fear          Avoid this situation


**SITUATION:** Being watched/observed when doing something/completing a task or activity

**ANXIETY LEVEL:**

**DO YOU:**     Face this fear          Avoid this situation

# ANXIETY Debrief

**Describe a situation where you felt anxious:**

**What were the physical symptoms you experienced?**

**Did you face the situation or remove yourself from it?**

**How did you cope with this anxiety?**
**Do you believe your thoughts and reactions were rational?**

# MOOD Chart

Use the wheel below to document your moods every month.
Use **3 different colors** to represent
positive, negative or neutral emotions.

POSITIVE          NEGATIVE          NEUTRAL

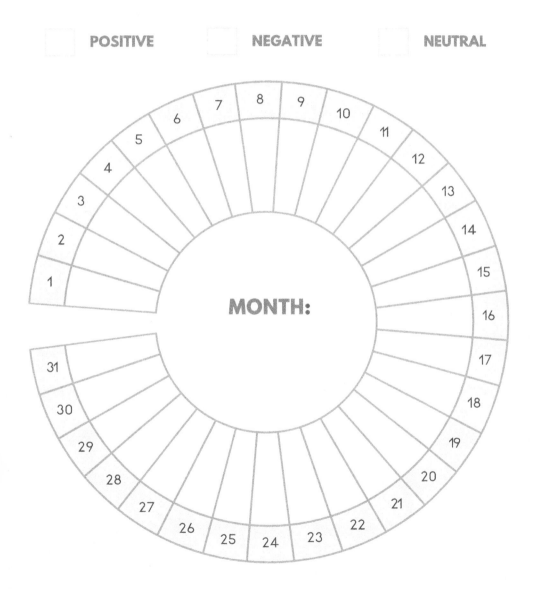

MONTH:

# TRIGGER Tracker

**Keep track of experiences that generate
negative thoughts and emotions.**

| DATE | INCIDENT | REACTION |
|------|----------|----------|
|      |          |          |
|      |          |          |
|      |          |          |
|      |          |          |
|      |          |          |
|      |          |          |
|      |          |          |
|      |          |          |
|      |          |          |
|      |          |          |

# SLEEP Tracker

Sleep plays a major factor in our ability to cope
with anxiety and depression.
Keep track of your sleep pattern in order to determine
how the amount of rest may be affecting your mental health.

| DAY | HOURS SLEPT | QUALITY OF SLEEP | THOUGHTS |
| --- | --- | --- | --- |
| 1 | | | |
| 2 | | | |
| 3 | | | |
| 4 | | | |
| 5 | | | |
| 6 | | | |
| 7 | | | |
| 8 | | | |
| 9 | | | |
| 10 | | | |
| 11 | | | |
| 12 | | | |
| 13 | | | |
| 14 | | | |
| 15 | | | |
| 16 | | | |
| 17 | | | |
| 18 | | | |
| 19 | | | |
| 20 | | | |
| 21 | | | |
| 22 | | | |
| 23 | | | |
| 24 | | | |
| 25 | | | |
| 26 | | | |
| 27 | | | |
| 28 | | | |
| 29 | | | |
| 30 | | | |
| 31 | | | |

# GRATEFUL Heart

| DAY | TODAY I AM GRATEFUL FOR: |
|-----|--------------------------|
| 1   |                          |
| 2   |                          |
| 3   |                          |
| 4   |                          |
| 5   |                          |
| 6   |                          |
| 7   |                          |
| 8   |                          |
| 9   |                          |
| 10  |                          |
| 11  |                          |
| 12  |                          |
| 13  |                          |
| 14  |                          |
| 15  |                          |
| 16  |                          |
| 17  |                          |
| 18  |                          |
| 19  |                          |
| 20  |                          |
| 21  |                          |
| 22  |                          |
| 23  |                          |
| 24  |                          |
| 25  |                          |
| 26  |                          |
| 27  |                          |
| 28  |                          |
| 29  |                          |
| 30  |                          |
| 31  |                          |

# SELF CARE Tracker

Self care is an important step in managing anxiety and depression.
It helps us recharge, reset and nurtures our mind and soul.
Focus on incorporating one self-care activity into your daily life.

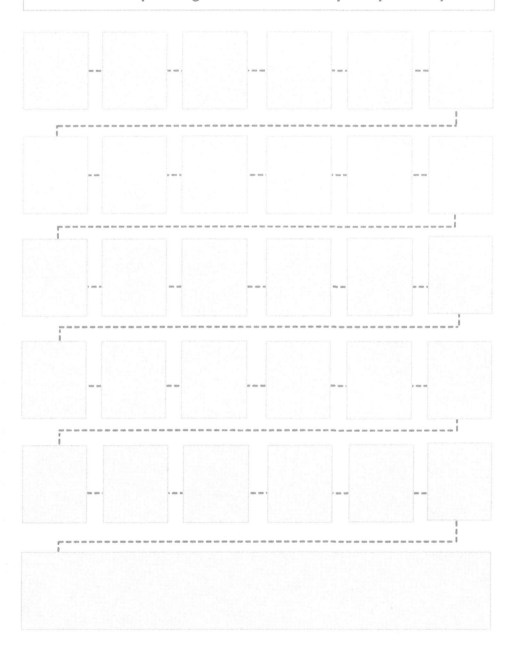

# THOUGHT Log

**Keep track of negative thoughts so you can
learn how to control irrational responses and triggers.**

| DATE | INCIDENT | INITIAL REACTION | RATIONAL REACTION |
|------|----------|------------------|-------------------|
|      |          |                  |                   |
|      |          |                  |                   |
|      |          |                  |                   |
|      |          |                  |                   |
|      |          |                  |                   |
|      |          |                  |                   |
|      |          |                  |                   |
|      |          |                  |                   |
|      |          |                  |                   |
|      |          |                  |                   |

# HAPPINESS Tracker

**Keep track of how often you feel happy and calm
and what you did to minimize negative responses.**

DATE:

HAPPINESS RATING: ☆☆☆☆☆

DATE:

HAPPINESS RATING: ☆☆☆☆☆

DATE:

HAPPINESS RATING: ☆☆☆☆☆

DATE:

HAPPINESS RATING: ☆☆☆☆☆

DATE:

HAPPINESS RATING: ☆☆☆☆☆

DATE:

HAPPINESS RATING: ☆☆☆☆☆

# PERSONAL *Wins*

It's important to celebrate both minor and major wins
when it comes to your mental health
and the coping strategies you've learned along the way.
You've come a long way!

## 2 RECENT WINS

| | |
|---|---|
| | |

## TOP 3 MILESTONES

| | |
|---|---|
| 1 | |
| 2 | |
| 3 | |

## 3 THINGS I'VE LEARNED ABOUT MYSELF OVER THE LAST YEAR

| | | |
|---|---|---|
| | | |

| PERSONAL REFLECTIONS | HOW I'VE LEARNED TO COPE WITH EMOTIONS |
|---|---|
| | |
| | |
| | |
| | |
| | |

## NOTES

| |
|---|
| |
| |
| |
| |
| |
| |
| |

# PERSONAL Rewards

**Make sure to reward yourself for accomplishments throughout your journey.
Whether it's a visit to your favorite restaurant, a bubble bath, or an evening with friends, it's important to celebrate your progress every step of the way.**

### IDEAS FOR PERSONAL REWARDS

| | |
|---|---|
| 1 | 2 |
| 3 | 4 |
| 5 | 6 |

| HOW I FELT BEFORE | HOW I REWARDED MYSELF | HOW I FELT AFTERWARD |
|---|---|---|
| | | |
| | | |
| | | |
| | | |
| | | |
| | | |
| | | |

| NOTES | PERSONAL REFLECTIONS/THOUGHTS |
|---|---|
| | |

137

# ANXIETY Tracker

MONTH:_____

**Document the days when you experienced anxiety.**

ANXIETY LEVELS (1-MILD, 10 SEVERE)                    NOTES

| | 01 | 02 | 03 | 04 | 05 | 06 | 07 | 08 | 09 | 10 | 11 | 12 |
|---|---|---|---|---|---|---|---|---|---|---|---|---|
| MON | 01 | 02 | 03 | 04 | 05 | 06 | 07 | 08 | 09 | 10 | 11 | 12 |
| TUE | 01 | 02 | 03 | 04 | 05 | 06 | 07 | 08 | 09 | 10 | 11 | 12 |
| WED | 01 | 02 | 03 | 04 | 05 | 06 | 07 | 08 | 09 | 10 | .11 | 12 |
| THU | 01 | 02 | 03 | 04 | 05 | 06 | 07 | 08 | 09 | 10 | 11 | 12 |
| FRI | 01 | 02 | 03 | 04 | 05 | 06 | 07 | 08 | 09 | 10 | 11 | 12 |
| SAT | 01 | 02 | 03 | 04 | 05 | 06 | 07 | 08 | 09 | 10 | 11 | 12 |
| SUN | 01 | 02 | 03 | 04 | 05 | 06 | 07 | 08 | 09 | 10 | 11 | 12 |

| | 01 | 02 | 03 | 04 | 05 | 06 | 07 | 08 | 09 | 10 | 11 | 12 |
|---|---|---|---|---|---|---|---|---|---|---|---|---|
| MON | 01 | 02 | 03 | 04 | 05 | 06 | 07 | 08 | 09 | 10 | 11 | 12 |
| TUE | 01 | 02 | 03 | 04 | 05 | 06 | 07 | 08 | 09 | 10 | 11 | 12 |
| WED | 01 | 02 | 03 | 04 | 05 | 06 | 07 | 08 | 09 | 10 | 11 | 12 |
| THU | 01 | 02 | 03 | 04 | 05 | 06 | 07 | 08 | 09 | 10 | 11 | 12 |
| FRI | 01 | 02 | 03 | 04 | 05 | 06 | 07 | 08 | 09 | 10 | 11 | 12 |
| SAT | 01 | 02 | 03 | 04 | 05 | 06 | 07 | 08 | 09 | 10 | 11 | 12 |
| SUN | 01 | 02 | 03 | 04 | 05 | 06 | 07 | 08 | 09 | 10 | 11 | 12 |

| | 01 | 02 | 03 | 04 | 05 | 06 | 07 | 08 | 09 | 10 | 11 | 12 |
|---|---|---|---|---|---|---|---|---|---|---|---|---|
| MON | 01 | 02 | 03 | 04 | 05 | 06 | 07 | 08 | 09 | 10 | 11 | 12 |
| TUE | 01 | 02 | 03 | 04 | 05 | 06 | 07 | 08 | 09 | 10 | 11 | 12 |
| WED | 01 | 02 | 03 | 04 | 05 | 06 | 07 | 08 | 09 | 10 | 11 | 12 |
| THU | 01 | 02 | 03 | 04 | 05 | 06 | 07 | 08 | 09 | 10 | 11 | 12 |
| FRI | 01 | 02 | 03 | 04 | 05 | 06 | 07 | 08 | 09 | 10 | 11 | 12 |
| SAT | 01 | 02 | 03 | 04 | 05 | 06 | 07 | 08 | 09 | 10 | 11 | 12 |
| SUN | 01 | 02 | 03 | 04 | 05 | 06 | 07 | 08 | 09 | 10 | 11 | 12 |

| | 01 | 02 | 03 | 04 | 05 | 06 | 07 | 08 | 09 | 10 | 11 | 12 |
|---|---|---|---|---|---|---|---|---|---|---|---|---|
| MON | 01 | 02 | 03 | 04 | 05 | 06 | 07 | 08 | 09 | 10 | 11 | 12 |
| TUE | 01 | 02 | 03 | 04 | 05 | 06 | 07 | 08 | 09 | 10 | 11 | 12 |
| WED | 01 | 02 | 03 | 04 | 05 | 06 | 07 | 08 | 09 | 10 | 11 | 12 |
| THU | 01 | 02 | 03 | 04 | 05 | 06 | 07 | 08 | 09 | 10 | 11 | 12 |
| FRI | 01 | 02 | 03 | 04 | 05 | 06 | 07 | 08 | 09 | 10 | 11 | 12 |
| SAT | 01 | 02 | 03 | 04 | 05 | 06 | 07 | 08 | 09 | 10 | 11 | 12 |
| SUN | 01 | 02 | 03 | 04 | 05 | 06 | 07 | 08 | 09 | 10 | 11 | 12 |

# DEPRESSION Tracker

**Document the days when you experienced depression.**

## DEPRESSION LEVELS (1-MILD, 10 SEVERE)                NOTES

| Day | | | | | | | | | | | | | Notes |
|---|---|---|---|---|---|---|---|---|---|---|---|---|---|
| MON | 01 | 02 | 03 | 04 | 05 | 06 | 07 | 08 | 09 | 10 | 11 | 12 | |
| TUE | 01 | 02 | 03 | 04 | 05 | 06 | 07 | 08 | 09 | 10 | 11 | 12 | |
| WED | 01 | 02 | 03 | 04 | 05 | 06 | 07 | 08 | 09 | 10 | 11 | 12 | |
| THU | 01 | 02 | 03 | 04 | 05 | 06 | 07 | 08 | 09 | 10 | 11 | 12 | |
| FRI | 01 | 02 | 03 | 04 | 05 | 06 | 07 | 08 | 09 | 10 | 11 | 12 | |
| SAT | 01 | 02 | 03 | 04 | 05 | 06 | 07 | 08 | 09 | 10 | 11 | 12 | |
| SUN | 01 | 02 | 03 | 04 | 05 | 06 | 07 | 08 | 09 | 10 | 11 | 12 | |
| MON | 01 | 02 | 03 | 04 | 05 | 06 | 07 | 08 | 09 | 10 | 11 | 12 | |
| TUE | 01 | 02 | 03 | 04 | 05 | 06 | 07 | 08 | 09 | 10 | 11 | 12 | |
| WED | 01 | 02 | 03 | 04 | 05 | 06 | 07 | 08 | 09 | 10 | 11 | 12 | |
| THU | 01 | 02 | 03 | 04 | 05 | 06 | 07 | 08 | 09 | 10 | 11 | 12 | |
| FRI | 01 | 02 | 03 | 04 | 05 | 06 | 07 | 08 | 09 | 10 | 11 | 12 | |
| SAT | 01 | 02 | 03 | 04 | 05 | 06 | 07 | 08 | 09 | 10 | 11 | 12 | |
| SUN | 01 | 02 | 03 | 04 | 05 | 06 | 07 | 08 | 09 | 10 | 11 | 12 | |
| MON | 01 | 02 | 03 | 04 | 05 | 06 | 07 | 08 | 09 | 10 | 11 | 12 | |
| TUE | 01 | 02 | 03 | 04 | 05 | 06 | 07 | 08 | 09 | 10 | 11 | 12 | |
| WED | 01 | 02 | 03 | 04 | 05 | 06 | 07 | 08 | 09 | 10 | 11 | 12 | |
| THU | 01 | 02 | 03 | 04 | 05 | 06 | 07 | 08 | 09 | 10 | 11 | 12 | |
| FRI | 01 | 02 | 03 | 04 | 05 | 06 | 07 | 08 | 09 | 10 | 11 | 12 | |
| SAT | 01 | 02 | 03 | 04 | 05 | 06 | 07 | 08 | 09 | 10 | 11 | 12 | |
| SUN | 01 | 02 | 03 | 04 | 05 | 06 | 07 | 08 | 09 | 10 | 11 | 12 | |
| MON | 01 | 02 | 03 | 04 | 05 | 06 | 07 | 08 | 09 | 10 | 11 | 12 | |
| TUE | 01 | 02 | 03 | 04 | 05 | 06 | 07 | 08 | 09 | 10 | 11 | 12 | |
| WED | 01 | 02 | 03 | 04 | 05 | 06 | 07 | 08 | 09 | 10 | 11 | 12 | |
| THU | 01 | 02 | 03 | 04 | 05 | 06 | 07 | 08 | 09 | 10 | 11 | 12 | |
| FRI | 01 | 02 | 03 | 04 | 05 | 06 | 07 | 08 | 09 | 10 | 11 | 12 | |
| SAT | 01 | 02 | 03 | 04 | 05 | 06 | 07 | 08 | 09 | 10 | 11 | 12 | |
| SUN | 01 | 02 | 03 | 04 | 05 | 06 | 07 | 08 | 09 | 10 | 11 | 12 | |

# DAILY *Reflection*

DATE: _____

### HOW I FEEL TODAY

### MY GREATEST CHALLENGE

### MOOD TRACKER:

MORNING:

EVENING:

I FELT HAPPY WHEN:

I FELT EXCITED WHEN:

I FELT ENERGIZED WHEN:

## Today's Highlights

## What I'm Grateful For Today

# DAILY Reflection

DATE: _____

HOW I FEEL TODAY

MY GREATEST CHALLENGE

MOOD TRACKER:

MORNING:

EVENING:

I FELT HAPPY WHEN:

I FELT EXCITED WHEN

I FELT ENERGIZED WHEN:

## Today's Highlights

## What I'm Grateful For Today

# DAILY Reflection

DATE: _____

## HOW I FEEL TODAY

## MY GREATEST CHALLENGE

## MOOD TRACKER:

MORNING:

EVENING:

I FELT HAPPY WHEN:

I FELT EXCITED WHEN:

I FELT ENERGIZED WHEN:

## Today's Highlights

## What I'm Grateful For Today

# DAILY Reflection

DATE: _____

HOW I FEEL TODAY

MY GREATEST CHALLENGE

MOOD TRACKER:

MORNING:

EVENING:

I FELT HAPPY WHEN:

I FELT EXCITED WHEN:

I FELT ENERGIZED WHEN:

## Today's Highlights

## What I'm Grateful For Today

# DAILY Reflection

DATE: _____

## HOW I FEEL TODAY

## MY GREATEST CHALLENGE

## MOOD TRACKER:

MORNING:

EVENING:

I FELT HAPPY WHEN:

I FELT EXCITED WHEN:

I FELT ENERGIZED WHEN:

## Today's Highlights

## What I'm Grateful For Today

# DAILY Reflection

DATE: _____

HOW I FEEL TODAY

MY GREATEST CHALLENGE

MOOD TRACKER:

MORNING:

EVENING:

I FELT HAPPY WHEN:

I FELT EXCITED WHEN:

I FELT ENERGIZED WHEN:

## Today's Highlights

## What I'm Grateful For Today

# DAILY Reflection

DATE: _____

HOW I FEEL TODAY

MY GREATEST CHALLENGE

MOOD TRACKER:

MORNING:

EVENING:

I FELT HAPPY WHEN:

I FELT EXCITED WHEN:

I FELT ENERGIZED WHEN:

## Today's Highlights

## What I'm Grateful For Today

# WEEKLY Assessment

WEEK OF:

|  | SLEEP | MOOD | POSITIVES | NEGATIVES |
|---|---|---|---|---|
| MONDAY |  |  |  |  |
| TUESDAY |  |  |  |  |
| WEDNESDAY |  |  |  |  |
| THURSDAY |  |  |  |  |
| FRIDAY |  |  |  |  |
| SATURADY |  |  |  |  |
| SUNDAY |  |  |  |  |

# POST THERAPY Chart

DATE:

## SUMMARY/OVERVIEW OF THERAPY SESSION

## WHAT WE DISCUSSED

## HOW IT MADE ME FEEL

## WHAT I LEARNED

## WHAT I WANT TO DISCUSS NEXT

**Rate your session to keep track of progress.**

SESSION SCORE

# DAILY Reflection

DATE: _____

HOW I FEEL TODAY

MY GREATEST CHALLENGE

MOOD TRACKER:

MORNING:

EVENING:

I FELT HAPPY WHEN:

I FELT EXCITED WHEN:

I FELT ENERGIZED WHEN:

## Today's Highlights

## What I'm Grateful For Today

# DAILY *Reflection*

DATE: _____

## HOW I FEEL TODAY

## MY GREATEST CHALLENGE

## MOOD TRACKER:

MORNING:

EVENING:

I FELT HAPPY WHEN:

I FELT EXCITED WHEN:

I FELT ENERGIZED WHEN:

## Today's Highlights

## What I'm Grateful For Today

# DAILY Reflection

DATE: _____

HOW I FEEL TODAY

MY GREATEST CHALLENGE

MOOD TRACKER:

MORNING:

EVENING:

I FELT HAPPY WHEN:

I FELT EXCITED WHEN:

I FELT ENERGIZED WHEN:

## Today's Highlights

## What I'm Grateful For Today

# DAILY Reflection

DATE: _____

HOW I FEEL TODAY

MY GREATEST CHALLENGE

MOOD TRACKER:

MORNING.

EVENING.

I FELT HAPPY WHEN:

I FELT EXCITED WHEN:

I FELT ENERGIZED WHEN:

## Today's Highlights

## What I'm Grateful For Today

# DAILY Reflection

DATE: _____

HOW I FEEL TODAY                     MY GREATEST CHALLENGE

MOOD TRACKER:

MORNING:                                          EVENING:

I FELT HAPPY WHEN:        I FELT EXCITED WHEN        I FELT ENERGIZED WHEN

## Today's Highlights

## What I'm Grateful For Today

# DAILY Reflection

DATE: _____

HOW I FEEL TODAY

MY GREATEST CHALLENGE

MOOD TRACKER:

MORNING:

EVENING:

I FELT HAPPY WHEN:

I FELT EXCITED WHEN:

I FELT ENERGIZED WHEN:

## Today's Highlights

## What I'm Grateful For Today

# DAILY Reflection

DATE: _____

HOW I FEEL TODAY                    MY GREATEST CHALLENGE

MOOD TRACKER:

MORNING:                            EVENING:

I FELT HAPPY WHEN:      I FELT EXCITED WHEN:      I FELT ENERGIZED WHEN:

## Today's Highlights

## What I'm Grateful For Today

# POST THERAPY Chart

DATE:

## SUMMARY/OVERVIEW OF THERAPY SESSION

## WHAT WE DISCUSSED

## HOW IT MADE ME FEEL

## WHAT I LEARNED

## WHAT I WANT TO DISCUSS NEXT

Rate your session to keep track of progress.

SESSION SCORE

# WEEKLY Assessment

WEEK OF:

| | SLEEP | MOOD | POSITIVES | NEGATIVES |
|---|---|---|---|---|
| MONDAY | | | | |
| TUESDAY | | | | |
| WEDNESDAY | | | | |
| THURSDAY | | | | |
| FRIDAY | | | | |
| SATURADY | | | | |
| SUNDAY | | | | |

# DAILY Reflection

DATE: _____

## HOW I FEEL TODAY

## MY GREATEST CHALLENGE

## MOOD TRACKER:

MORNING:

EVENING:

I FELT HAPPY WHEN:

I FELT EXCITED WHEN:

I FELT ENERGIZED WHEN:

## Today's Highlights

## What I'm Grateful For Today

# DAILY Reflection

DATE: _____

HOW I FEEL TODAY                    MY GREATEST CHALLENGE

MOOD TRACKER:

MORNING:                            EVENING:

I FELT HAPPY WHEN:      I FELT EXCITED WHEN:      I FELT ENERGIZED WHEN:

## Today's Highlights

## What I'm Grateful For Today

# DAILY *Reflection*

DATE: _____

## HOW I FEEL TODAY

## MY GREATEST CHALLENGE

## MOOD TRACKER:

MORNING:

EVENING:

I FELT HAPPY WHEN:

I FELT EXCITED WHEN:

I FELT ENERGIZED WHEN:

## Today's Highlights

## What I'm Grateful For Today

# DAILY *Reflection*

HOW I FEEL TODAY

MY GREATEST CHALLENGE

MOOD TRACKER:

MORNING:

EVENING:

I FELT HAPPY WHEN:

I FELT EXCITED WHEN:

I FELT ENERGIZED WHEN:

## Today's Highlights

## What I'm Grateful For Today

# DAILY Reflection

DATE: _____

## HOW I FEEL TODAY

## MY GREATEST CHALLENGE

## MOOD TRACKER:

MORNING.

EVENING:

I FELT HAPPY WHEN:

I FELT EXCITED WHEN:

I FELT ENERGIZED WHEN:

### Today's Highlights

### What I'm Grateful For Today

# DAILY Reflection

DATE: _____

HOW I FEEL TODAY

MY GREATEST CHALLENGE

MOOD TRACKER:

MORNING:

EVENING:

I FELT HAPPY WHEN:

I FELT EXCITED WHEN:

I FELT ENERGIZED WHEN:

## Today's Highlights

## What I'm Grateful For Today

# DAILY Reflection

DATE: _____

### HOW I FEEL TODAY

### MY GREATEST CHALLENGE

### MOOD TRACKER:

MORNING:

EVENING:

I FELT HAPPY WHEN:

I FELT EXCITED WHEN:

I FELT ENERGIZED WHEN:

## Today's Highlights

## What I'm Grateful For Today

# WEEKLY Assessment

WEEK OF:

| | SLEEP | MOOD | POSITIVES | NEGATIVES |
|---|---|---|---|---|
| MONDAY | | | | |
| TUESDAY | | | | |
| WEDNESDAY | | | | |
| THURSDAY | | | | |
| FRIDAY | | | | |
| SATURADY | | | | |
| SUNDAY | | | | |

# POST THERAPY *Chart*

DATE:

### SUMMARY/OVERVIEW OF THERAPY SESSION

### WHAT WE DISCUSSED

### HOW IT MADE ME FEEL

### WHAT I LEARNED

### WHAT I WANT TO DISCUSS NEXT

**Rate your session to keep track of progress.**

SESSION SCORE

166

# DAILY *Reflection*

DATE: _____

HOW I FEEL TODAY                           MY GREATEST CHALLENGE

MOOD TRACKER:

MORNING:                                         EVENING:

I FELT HAPPY WHEN:          I FELT EXCITED WHEN:          I FELT ENERGIZED WHEN:

*Today's Highlights*

*What I'm Grateful For Today*

# DAILY Reflection

DATE: _____

HOW I FEEL TODAY

MY GREATEST CHALLENGE

MOOD TRACKER:

MORNING.

EVENING:

I FELT HAPPY WHEN:

I FELT EXCITED WHEN:

I FELT ENERGIZED WHEN:

## Today's Highlights

## What I'm Grateful For Today

# DAILY Reflection

DATE: _____

HOW I FEEL TODAY

MY GREATEST CHALLENGE

MOOD TRACKER:

MORNING:

EVENING:

I FELT HAPPY WHEN:

I FELT EXCITED WHEN:

I FELT ENERGIZED WHEN:

## Today's Highlights

## What I'm Grateful For Today

# DAILY *Reflection*

DATE: _____

HOW I FEEL TODAY

MY GREATEST CHALLENGE

MOOD TRACKER:

MORNING:

EVENING:

I FELT HAPPY WHEN:

I FELT EXCITED WHEN:

I FELT ENERGIZED WHEN:

## Today's Highlights

## What I'm Grateful For Today

# DAILY Reflection

DATE: _____

HOW I FEEL TODAY

MY GREATEST CHALLENGE

MOOD TRACKER:

MORNING:

EVENING:

I FELT HAPPY WHEN:

I FELT EXCITED WHEN:

I FELT ENERGIZED WHEN:

## Today's Highlights

## What I'm Grateful For Today

# DAILY Reflection

DATE: _____

HOW I FEEL TODAY

MY GREATEST CHALLENGE

MOOD TRACKER:

MORNING:

EVENING:

I FELT HAPPY WHEN:

I FELT EXCITED WHEN:

I FELT ENERGIZED WHEN:

## Today's Highlights

## What I'm Grateful For Today

# DAILY *Reflection*

DATE: _____

HOW I FEEL TODAY

MY GREATEST CHALLENGE

MOOD TRACKER:

MORNING:

EVENING:

I FELT HAPPY WHEN:

I FELT EXCITED WHEN:

I FELT ENERGIZED WHEN:

## Today's Highlights

## What I'm Grateful For Today

# POST THERAPY *Chart*

DATE:

## SUMMARY/OVERVIEW OF THERAPY SESSION

### WHAT WE DISCUSSED

### HOW IT MADE ME FEEL

### WHAT I LEARNED

### WHAT I WANT TO DISCUSS NEXT

**Rate your session to keep track of progress.**

SESSION SCORE

# WEEKLY Assessment

WEEK OF:

| | SLEEP | MOOD | POSITIVES | NEGATIVES |
|---|---|---|---|---|
| MONDAY | | | | |
| TUESDAY | | | | |
| WEDNESDAY | | | | |
| THURSDAY | | | | |
| FRIDAY | | | | |
| SATURADY | | | | |
| SUNDAY | | | | |

# DAILY *Reflection*

DATE: _____

HOW I FEEL TODAY

MY GREATEST CHALLENGE

MOOD TRACKER:

MORNING:

EVENING:

I FELT HAPPY WHEN:

I FELT EXCITED WHEN:

I FELT ENERGIZED WHEN:

## Today's Highlights

## What I'm Grateful For Today

# DAILY Reflection

DATE: _____

HOW I FEEL TODAY                    MY GREATEST CHALLENGE

MOOD TRACKER:

MORNING:                                    EVENING:

I FELT HAPPY WHEN:        I FELT EXCITED WHEN        I FELT ENERGIZED WHEN:

## Today's Highlights

## What I'm Grateful For Today

# DAILY Reflection

DATE: _____

HOW I FEEL TODAY

MY GREATEST CHALLENGE

MOOD TRACKER:

MORNING:

EVENING:

I FELT HAPPY WHEN:

I FELT EXCITED WHEN:

I FELT ENERGIZED WHEN:

## Today's Highlights

## What I'm Grateful For Today

# ANXIETY Levels

**Use the chart below to rate your level of anxiety when facing various situations by coloring the boxes:**

**SITUATION:**   Meeting someone new

**ANXIETY LEVEL:**

**DO YOU:**   Face this fear       Avoid this situation


**SITUATION:**   Going shopping or to the grocery store

**ANXIETY LEVEL:**

**DO YOU:**   Face this fear       Avoid this situation


**SITUATION:**   Stating your opinion when potentially controversial or opposing

**ANXIETY LEVEL:**

**DO YOU:**   Face this fear       Avoid this situation


**SITUATION:**   Standing up for yourself when treated unfairly or poorly

**ANXIETY LEVEL:**

**DO YOU:**   Face this fear       Avoid this situation


**SITUATION:**   Spending time alone with friends and/or family

**ANXIETY LEVEL:**

**DO YOU:**   Face this fear       Avoid this situation


**SITUATION:**   Being watched/observed when doing something/completing a task or activity

**ANXIETY LEVEL:**

**DO YOU:**   Face this fear       Avoid this situation

# ANXIETY Debrief

**Describe a situation where you felt anxious:**

**What were the physical symptoms you experienced?**

**Did you face the situation or remove yourself from it?**

**How did you cope with this anxiety?**
**Do you believe your thoughts and reactions were rational?**

Made in the USA
Las Vegas, NV
23 January 2024

84791520R00105